STONE AGE

Written by Anita Ganeri

W
FRANKLIN WATTS
LONDON • SYDNEY

Franklin Watts
First published in Great Britain in 2018
by The Watts Publishing Group
Copyright © The Watts Publishing Group, 2018
All rights reserved.

Editors: Sarah Ridley and Sarah Silver
Designer: Matt Lilly
Picture researcher: Diana Morris

ISBN 978 1 4451 5310 0

FSC
www.fsc.org
MIX
Paper from
responsible sources
FSC® C104740

Printed in China

Franklin Watts
An imprint of
Hachette Children's Group
Part of The Watts Publishing Group
Carmelite House
50 Victoria Embankment
London EC4Y 0DZ

An Hachette UK Company
www.hachette.co.uk

www.franklinwatts.co.uk

Contents

What was the Stone Age?

The Stone Age began around 2.5 million years ago, and it lasted until about 4,500 years ago. It is the longest period in prehistory, the time before people used a written language. The Stone Age is often divided into three parts: Palaeolithic (Old Stone Age), Mesolithic (Middle Stone Age) and Neolithic (New Stone Age).

An artist's impression of a Stone Age hunting camp in Happisburgh, Norfolk, 900,000 years ago, soon after humans arrived in Britain.

Stones and bones

The Stone Age got its name because, at that time, people made their tools and weapons from stone, as well as bone. Towards the end of the Stone Age, people learned how to make things from metal – first copper, and then bronze. This discovery transformed people's lives and marked the end of the Stone Age and the beginning of the Bronze Age.

The Stone Age

Around 2.5 million–10,000 BCE	Palaeolithic (Old Stone Age)
Around 10,000–4000 BCE	Mesolithic (Middle Stone Age)
Around 4000–2400 BCE	Neolithic (New Stone Age)
Around 2400–800 BCE	Bronze Age

BCE means 'before the Common Era' and is used to show the number of years before Jesus was born in the first century, which can also be indicated using the letters BC (before Christ). So, for instance, 4000 BCE was over 6,000 years ago.

PREHISTORIC EVIDENCE

There are no written records from the Stone Age. However, archaeologists have made many spectacular finds, including paintings, tools, tombs, houses, bones and even long-dead bodies, that have helped them to build up a picture of how prehistoric people lived. Although writing had not yet been invented, people expressed themselves with art painted on cave walls, and symbols carved on stone and bone.

WRITING HISTORY

Throughout this book, you will find panels asking you to write your own versions of the history you have read. You will find the information you need in the book, but you can also look online and in other books. Use the tips provided, and don't be afraid to let your imagination run wild.

Stone Age cave art from Altamira, Spain showing a red deer. It was painted about 22,000 years ago.

Life in the Stone Age

Humans probably first arrived in Britain around a million years ago, when it was joined to Europe by a wide bridge of land. The earliest evidence we have for them is a set of human footprints left in the mud around 900,000 years ago. During this time, people had to cope with extreme changes of climate and were forced to leave Britain when conditions became extremely cold, returning in warmer times.

First people

The ancestors of modern humans (*Homo sapiens*) originally came from Africa. By about 40,000 years ago, they were living across Europe, eventually arriving in Britain.

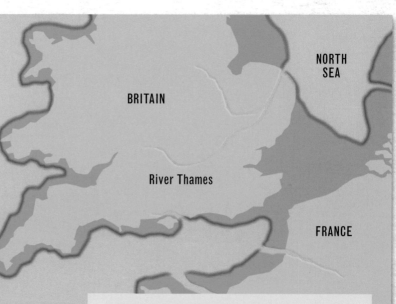

NORTH SEA

BRITAIN

River Thames

FRANCE

This map shows Britain and Europe about 900,000 years ago, when Britain was not an island. Animals, including people, travelled back and forth across a land bridge.

The 400,000-year-old skull of a woman was found in Swanscombe, Kent in England.

For a while, they lived alongside another group of early humans, called Neanderthals. The Neanderthals were short and stockily built, which helped them to cope with the cold. They later died out, and disappeared from Britain.

Did you know?

Some archaeologists have been working to reconstruct the faces of Stone Age people. First, they make a 3-D model of the original skull, then add muscles and tissues in clay. They use this model to make a mould which they fill with silicone to form a head. Finally, they add features, such as hair.

This reconstruction is based on a 5,500-year-old skeleton found at Stonehenge, England.

Changing climate

During the Stone Age, the climate changed between hot and cold. Every 100,000 years or so, it grew so cold that vast ice sheets covered large parts of the world, including Britain and Europe. These cold spells are called Ice Ages and were followed by warmer periods when animals, such as lions and rhinos, roamed Europe, and hippos swam in the River Thames. At the end of the last Ice Age, around 6,500 BCE, so much ice melted across the world that sea waters flooded the land bridge, making Britain into an island.

Write a Stone Age weather report

Write a short newspaper weather report for Britain during an Ice Age or a warmer period. Look in a newspaper to see how to set out your report and what sort of information you need to include.

Stone Age tools

Stone Age people were skilled at making tools out of stone, especially flint. They chipped the flint into shape, using a harder rock as a hammer. This is called flint knapping. Some of the earliest tools were hand axes. These had sharp edges for cutting, and a round base for fitting in your hand. Hand axes were used for digging up roots, cutting meat and scraping animal skins clean.

cutting edge

A hand axe made from flint.

Flint mine

In the 19th century, an extraordinary flint mine was found in East Anglia, England. It is called Grimes Graves. Around 5,000 years ago, miners dug more than 430 shafts, using picks and shovels made from deer antlers and ox bones. Simple wooden ladders led down into the mine, where working conditions were dark, cramped and dangerous. The flints they mined were made into tools and weapons.

An illustration of miners at work in Grimes Graves flint mine about 5,000 years ago.

Write a job advert for a flint miner

Imagine that you are in charge of recruiting people to work in Grimes Graves. Write an advert describing the work and conditions, and the types of people you are looking for. Look at some job adverts in newspapers or online to help you.

At Skara Brae, people made their houses from stone as there was plenty about. They built them partly below ground for warmth.

Stone Age village

Early in the Stone Age, people followed the animals they hunted, sleeping in makeshift shelters or caves. Much later, they began to build houses and settle in one place. These homes were usually built from wood, mud and reeds. However, in Orkney, there are the ruins of a stone-built Neolithic village at Skara Brae. Built around 5,000 years ago, it has eight stone houses and a workshop, originally roofed in thick turf. Each house has a large, square room, with a stone fireplace, stone beds around the walls and a stone cupboard, probably used to display special objects.

DIG DIARY

Skara Brae was first discovered in 1850 when a fierce winter storm stripped the grass from a large mound, revealing the stone buildings. From 1928–30, the site was thoroughly excavated by archaeologist, Vere Gordon Childe. He produced a huge number of writings about his work, including books, journals and notebooks.

Ice man discovery

On 19 September 1991, two German tourists, Helmut and Erika Simon, were hiking in the Alps when they made an extraordinary find. Coming down the mountain, they noticed a head and shoulders sticking out of the ice. The couple thought that they had stumbled across the remains of a missing climber, caught in a recent avalanche. In fact, they had discovered the body of a prehistoric man.

The walkers with their discovery — the body of Ötzi sticking out of the ice.

About Ötzi

The body was removed from the ice and taken to the University of Innsbruck where experts began to examine it. They quickly realised the importance of the find. Nicknamed Ötzi, the man was estimated to have been about 1.65 m tall, and to have been around 45 years old when he died. He wore clothes made from animal skins, with a cloak of woven grass, and had more than 60 tattoos.

A museum reconstruction of how Ötzi may have looked.

Did you know?

From the style of copper axe that Ötzi carried, experts estimate that he lived around 5,000 years ago. He lived between the end of the Stone Age and the start of the Bronze Age, at a time when human beings were beginning to use metal for the first time.

Writing History: Eyewitness account

Imagine that you are one of the tourists who discovered Ötzi. Write an eyewitness account of finding his body half-hidden in the ice. Describe how you felt when you first saw it. What did you think that you had found? Were you surprised when archaeologists confirmed that the body dated back thousands of years? The opening few lines have been written for you.

September 1991

Ötztal Alps, Austria/Italy

We'd spent all day hiking in the Alps, and were heading down the mountain on our way back home. Helmut was walking ahead of me when he shouted out that he'd spotted something poking out of the glacier. It looked like a body, lying face down in the ice.

WRITING HINTS AND TIPS

- Arrange your account in chronological order (the order in which it happened).
- Use descriptive language to paint a vivid picture for your reader.
- Remember to tell the reader how you felt about what happened.
- Organise your account into paragraphs to make it easier to read.
- Unless you know your reader, use quite formal language.

Finding food

A herd of modern-day reindeer.

In the early Stone Age, people moved from place to place, looking for food. They were hunter-gatherers, collecting wild nuts, berries, fruit and roots. They hunted animals, such as reindeer, wild horses, deer and wild boar, and they also caught fish and birds. As the herds of animals moved to new grazing areas, people followed after them. They travelled on foot, over huge distances, and lived in different camps and caves throughout the year.

Waste not, want not

Hunting an animal, such as a reindeer, was hard work, and people made the most of any catch. No part of the animal was wasted. A reindeer's antlers were used to make tools and weapons. The skin was made into clothes, tents and bags. Once the meat was cut off the bones, they were smashed to get the fat-rich bone marrow. The tongue, nose, eyeballs, liver and kidneys were also rich in protein and fat.

In the Stone Age, some people lived in tents similar to these made by Siberian reindeer herders using reindeer skin and branches.

For hunting, early Stone Age people used sharpened sticks. Later, in the Mesolithic period, people used spears and harpoons. One of the most important tools was a tiny, sharp piece of flint, called a microlith. Microliths were made from flakes of flint, carefully chipped to a very sharp point which inflicted a deep, cutting wound.

They were fixed to sticks to make hunting weapons, possibly using tree resin or twine. Around 6–18 microliths might have been used on one spear or harpoon. Another invention was the spear-thrower, carved from wood or reindeer antler. It allowed hunters to hurl their spears as far as 250 m.

Some microliths are only a few millimetres long while others are up to 3 cm long.

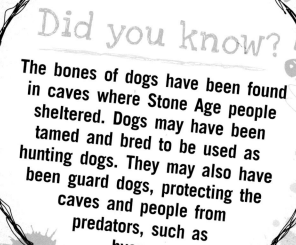

Did you know?

The bones of dogs have been found in caves where Stone Age people sheltered. Dogs may have been tamed and bred to be used as hunting dogs. They may also have been guard dogs, protecting the caves and people from predators, such as hyenas.

Mammoth hunters

Normally, Stone Age people hunted animals such as deer and horses, but they also hunted mammoths. Mammoths were large and dangerous, and hunting them brought many risks, especially as hunters were only armed with spears. Young, sick or single animals were probably targeted because they were easier to kill. They were chased into muddy swamps, where they became trapped, or were driven over the edge of a cliff.

Paintings and carvings of mammoths and other animals were made on the walls of Rouffignac Cave, France, about 13,000 years ago.

Did you know?

At the World Mammoth Centre in Russia, scientists are working hard to bring the mammoth back to life. They are taking DNA from mammoth remains, and copying the genes. Hopefully, this will, one day, make it possible for them to create a living mammoth.

Mammoth remains

Mammoths became extinct around 4,000 years ago, as a result of climate change and hunting by humans. But mammoth remains are regularly found in the frozen ground of Siberia, Russia. In 2013, an almost complete mammoth body was dug up, including its trunk and tusks. Carbon dating showed that it was 40,000 years old. It had most likely become stuck in a peat bog and was then killed by wolves.

Mammoth bone huts

In 1965, a farmer in Mezhyrich, Ukraine, was excavating a cellar under his house, when he dug up a mammoth jawbone. He had stumbled on the ruins of four huts, made from mammoth bones, dating back some 15,000 years. Inside, there were other incredible finds, including a drum made from a mammoth skull.

A reconstruction of one of the mammoth-bone huts found in Ukraine shown at an exhibition held in Japan.

Building bones

Hunters built the huts from mammoth bones because there were no trees or caves to shelter in. First, they made a ring of interlocking jawbones to form a solid base. Then, about 36 huge, curved tusks were used to make an arch to support the roof and porch. Finally, the whole frame was covered in mammoth hides.

Write an estate agent's blurb

You're a mammoth hunter from the Ukraine, and you're looking to sell your mammoth bone hut. Write an estate agent's blurb. Give plenty of details, including its size and location, as well as picking out its best features, such as the fact that it is so solidly built that it will last for years and years. Look online to find out how to lay out your blurb.

Writing History: A mammoth hunter's blog

Imagine that you are a Stone Age mammoth hunter, setting out on your first mammoth hunt. Write a blog about what happens from day to day. Describe what happens during the day, and how you feel about it. Are you scared when you see a mammoth up close for the first time? The first post has been written for you.

WRITING HINTS AND TIPS

- Write your blog in chronological order (the order in which things happen).

- Put yourself in the hunter's place and write your blog in the first person.

- Describe the things that happen but also how you feel about them.

- You can use informal language for blogs – keep it friendly and casual.

- Read blogs written by other people to help you improve your style.

First day

Set off this morning, at first light, following the mammoth tracks we spotted a few days ago. I'm so excited! I've been waiting for ages to go on my first mammoth hunt. It's scary, too – I've never seen a mammoth up close. Anyway, we're all really hungry so I hope it doesn't get away.

First farmers

Around 11,000 years ago, people in the Middle East started to grow crops and keep animals. As knowledge about farming spread, people began to build permanent homes and settle in one place. This marked a new period of prehistory during the Stone Age, known as the Neolithic Age.

At Stonehenge, England, you can see reconstructions of five Neolithic houses.

Farming Britain

Farming reached Britain around 6,000 years ago, probably introduced by people arriving from Europe by boat. They brought animals, such as sheep, goats and cattle, together with seeds to plant, and the tools needed for digging and harvesting. Slowly, people cleared forests to make space for growing crops, such as wheat and barley, and for their animals to graze. They kept and bred wild boar and eventually farmed them as pigs.

Write an interview

Write down an interview with a Stone Age farmer. Start by thinking of five questions that you might like to ask. For example, you could ask the farmer which crops are easiest to grow or which animals he likes to keep. Keep your questions short and snappy. Now write the farmer's answers, which can be longer and fuller.

The ancestors of the Manx Loaghtan sheep date back to the earliest days of British farming.

Arts and crafts

Although Stone Age people did not have a written language, they were skilled artists, creating beautiful paintings, carvings and sculptures. These were often of the animals they hunted, and were produced on stone slabs, antlers and mammoth ivory, as well as on cave walls. People may have believed that these works of art would bring them success in the hunt.

Animal carvings

Animal carvings have been found all over Europe. In 1866, an amazing carving was discovered in France. It was broken into two pieces. When these were fitted together, they formed a single sculpture of two reindeer, swimming nose to tail. The sculpture may have been designed to communicate with the spirit world or to bring good luck on a hunt, but no one knows for sure. Today, the sculpture is on display in the British Museum in London, UK.

A Stone Age artist carved these swimming reindeer from a mammoth tusk about 13,000 years ago.

SIGNS AND SYMBOLS

The walls of the Pech Merle Cave in France (see page 21) are decorated with bison, mammoths, horses and handprints, as well as symbols, such as triangles, circles, crosses and branch-like shapes. They date from around 30,000 years ago. Archaeologists think that the symbols are arranged in patterns, like a code, and that they may have been a very early form of writing.

Some unusual carved stone balls (right) were found at Skara Brae in Orkney (see page 9). Each ball was covered in carved knobs. Using only stone tools, they took great skill and patience to make. They were probably symbols of power that showed off their owner's importance.

Stone balls found at Skara Brae in Orkney, Scotland.

Stone Age jewellery

Stone Age people may have painted their bodies and braided their hair with shells and feathers. They also wore jewellery, made from materials such as stones, shells, teeth and bones. A 35,000-year-old bead-making factory has been found in France. Here, mammoth tusks and soapstone were turned into tens of thousands of tiny beads.

A Neolithic necklace made from green stones, found near the stone circle at Almendres, Portugal.

Cave art

Some of the most spectacular works of Stone Age art have been found on the walls and floors of caves. They show many different animals, particularly the ones people hunted, such as reindeer, bison, mammoths, and horses. No one knows for certain if this art had a special meaning, but it may have been intended to bring good luck when hunting.

This bird's head is one of about 80 Stone Age carvings at Cresswell Crags caves. It is at least 12,000 years old.

Artists' tools

Stone Age artists used paints made from natural materials, such as ground down rocks or plant roots, mixed with water or animal fat. Outlines were drawn, using charcoal or soot from the fire.

Paints came in three basic colours – red, from ochre or haematite, yellow from goethite, and black from charcoal or manganese. To apply the paints, they used their fingers or sticks.

A stone and a shell from Blombos Cave, used to make paint during the Stone Age.

Did you know?

At Blombos Cave in South Africa, archaeologists discovered a Stone Age ochre workshop. Among the artists' tools were two large shells, used for mixing and storing paint, stones, used for grinding the ochre, and bones, used for stirring.

Handy prints

Many cave walls were covered in colourful handprints. These were produced in two ways. For a print, a person painted their hand, then pressed it onto the rock. For a stencil, a person placed their hand on the rock. Then they blew paint over it through a hollow bone or reed.

Hand stencils around horses painted in the Pech Merle Cave in France around 30,000 years ago.

Artists' signatures?

Experts are still trying to work out why the handprints were made. They may have been used as artists' signatures or as a way of communicating in the darkness of the cave. The position of the prints may have given useful information, such as how to move safely through the passageways.

Write a how-to guide to cave art

Write a short how-to guide to creating a piece of Stone Age cave art, such as a painting of a mammoth, or a group of handprints. Write a list of tools and materials, then a list of step-by-step instructions.

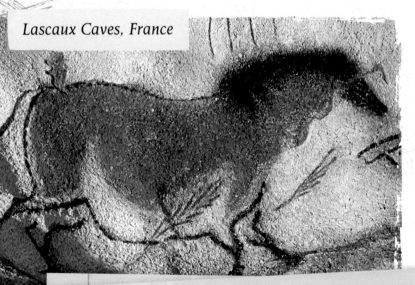

Famous cave

Some of the greatest works of Stone Age art are found in the Lascaux Caves in France. Hundreds of extraordinary paintings, around 17,000 years old, cover the cave walls and ceilings. The paintings mostly show large animals, most famously in the Hall of the Bulls. Here, there are horses, stags and huge bulls, one more than 5 m long.

Lascaux Caves, France

Amazing discovery

For thousands of years, the caves and their artwork lay hidden. Then, on 12 September 1940, four boys stumbled on a small hole, made the previous winter, when an oak tree had been uprooted in a storm. The boys made the hole bigger, and found that, to their astonishment, it led to a long passageway. At the end lay a large cavern, covered in brilliantly coloured paintings.

Make a Stone Age cartoon

Stone Age people used art as a way of telling stories. Create a cartoon strip, showing a mammoth or reindeer hunt. Draw the pictures in the style of the Stone Age, using Stone Age colours. Write a short piece of text for each picture frame to say what is happening, and use speech or thought bubbles to help move the action along.

News report

At first, the boys kept their discovery secret, but eventually told their teacher who contacted an expert. Imagine that you are a journalist, sent to investigate the breaking story. As part of your article, you visit the site of the caves, and also interview the boys. Here are the opening lines to get you started:

THE DAILY CAVE

26 SEPTEMBER 1940

LASCAUX, FRANCE

BOYS IN GREATEST EVER ART FIND!

The entrance to the cave with two of the boys, Marcel Ravidat and Jacques Marsal, their teacher (left) and Henri Breuil, the expert (right).

Four friends from a nearby village are still reeling after stumbling across a prehistoric art gallery a fortnight ago.

"It was so amazing," one of the boys told me. "We didn't want anyone else to see it so we kept it a secret until now."

WRITING HINTS AND TIPS

- Begin your article with a catchy headline to grab your readers' attention.
- The opening paragraph should be an introduction to the story.
- Don't give too much away at first. Keep building up the suspense.
- Interviews with eyewitnesses help to bring your story to life.
- Look at a newspaper in print or on-line to get some ideas.

Stone Age beliefs

From around 40,000 years ago, Stone Age people are believed to have carried out special rituals and ceremonies to mark important events in their lives. Many of these centred around hunting and death.

A deer's skull with antlers found at Star Carr in North Yorkshire, England.

Hunting rituals

Star Carr in North Yorkshire, England dates from around 11,000 years ago. It was a Stone Age hunting camp, used during the winter to hunt deer. Here, archaeologists have found 21 deer skulls, with the antlers still attached. Two holes were cut into each skull, and the inside of the skull rubbed smooth. Experts think that hunters may have worn the skulls to disguise themselves while out hunting, or as part of a ritual to bring good luck in the hunt.

Write an acrostic poem

Try writing an acrostic poem using the word 'HUNTING'. It could be read out at a Stone Age ceremony. Write the letters of the word in a line down the side of the page. Then use the first letter of each line to start a word or phrase.

Standing stones

Towards the end of the Stone Age, people began to build impressive circles of stone. Several stone circles are still standing today. The Ring of Brodgar in Orkney was originally made up of 60 stones, up to 4.7 m tall. It stands on a narrow strip of land between two lochs (seawater lakes). Its spectacular setting, combined with the enormous effort put into building it, show that it was a very important place. It may have been used for religious rituals, as a meeting place, or for studying the stars.

The Ring of Brodgar in Orkney, Scotland.

Write a Stone Age postcard

It is late in the Stone Age, and you are visiting the Ring of Brodgar with your family. Write a postcard to a friend back home, telling them about what you have seen. You haven't got much space, so make sure that you pick out the most important points. You could draw the Ring of Brodgar on the other side of your card.

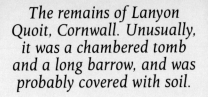

West Kennet Long Barrow in Wiltshire, England.

Burying the dead

Neanderthals (see page 6) may have been the first people to take care how they buried their dead, placing precious objects in their graves. Much later, people built huge mounds, called long barrows, where large numbers of people from the same community could be buried together. West Kennet long barrow in England was built around 5,600 years ago. A long mound of earth, it has several stone burial chambers inside, where the remains of 50 people were found.

The remains of Lanyon Quoit, Cornwall. Unusually, it was a chambered tomb and a long barrow, and was probably covered with soil.

Passage tombs

Newgrange in Ireland is one of the most remarkable Stone Age tombs. Built around 5,200 years ago, it is covered in a circular mound of earth, stones and grass. A stone circle stands around it. Inside, a long passage leads to a central burial chamber, with three smaller chambers leading off it.

Some of the stone slabs lining the walls are covered in swirling artwork. The tomb was designed so that, every year, at dawn on the shortest day, the sunlight shines through a hole above the entrance, straight into the main chamber.

The outer wall of Newgrange has been largely rebuilt to show how it would have looked.

Swirling patterns on a stone slab at Newgrange, Ireland.

SWIRLING PATTERNS

The entrance stone to Newgrange and some of the stone slabs lining the walls of the burial chamber are covered in swirling art. When the stones were in place, Neolithic people carved the designs using a sharp point. No one knows what they mean today but at the time they were created, people may have understood.

The Red Lady of Paviland

In January 1823, William Buckland, professor of geology at Oxford University, made an astonishing discovery. While excavating in Goat's Hole Cave, Paviland, Wales, he came across a body. Its bones were stained red with ochre and it was surrounded by rods and bracelets, made from mammoth tusks, and bracelets made from periwinkle shells.

Goat's Hole Cave in Paviland, Wales.

Mistakenly, Buckland thought that this was the body of a Roman woman, but later research showed that it was a man in his 20s or 30s. He had died around 30,000 years ago, during the Palaeolithic period, and had been buried in the cave with a mammoth skull. He may have been a hunter, killed during a hunt, or he may have been an important chief or religious leader. No one knows for sure.

Surviving bones of the Red Lady of Paviland, now known to belong to a man.

Did you know?

When scientists analysed the bones found in the cave, they found that he lived on a diet made up of fish, horse, reindeer, roots and berries, and had been in good health when he died. It may be that his body was brought from the coast to the special burial site of the cave.

Writing History: A letter home

Put yourself in the place of William Buckland. You have spent the week in Wales, exploring Goat's Hole Cave and you can't wait to tell people about your amazing discovery. Write a letter home to your wife, Mary – the opening has already been written for you. Pack the letter with information, but also remember to tell her how you feel about what you have found.

Goat's Hole Cave
Paviland
Gower
Wales

27th January 1823

My dearest Mary,

I've got so much to tell you, I don't know where to start. This has been the most exciting week of my life. True, I've spent most of it on my hands and knees, but wait until I tell you what I've found. Never mind mammoth bones, I found a human body, buried in the cave!

William Buckland
(1784–1856)

WRITING HINTS AND TIPS

- If you're writing to someone you know, you can use friendly, informal language.
- Use more formal language if you're writing to someone you don't know.
- Find out the correct way of laying out formal and informal letters.
- Make notes about what you want to say before you start your letter.
- Read through your letter before sending it, to check for any mistakes.

Glossary

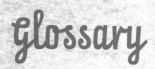

ancestor Early humans or relatives who died a long time ago.

archaeologist A person who studies the past from objects and other evidence left behind.

bronze A metal made from mixing copper and tin.

burial chamber A room underground or inside a building where a dead body is placed.

carbon dating A way of telling how old an object is by measuring the amount of carbon it contains.

charcoal A black material made by heating wood.

climate The weather that a place has over a long period of time.

community A group of people that live together and share common interests.

copper A soft metal with a reddish-brown colour.

crop A plant that is grown in fields for food, such as wheat or oats.

DNA A chemical pattern like a signature, found in living cells and passed on from one generation to the next.

estate agent A person who helps people to buy and sell a house.

excavate To dig up from the ground.

extinct When a living thing dies out completely, leaving none of that species alive anywhere in the world.

genes Parts of your cells that carry information about your features and characteristics.

glacier A long river of ice that moves very slowly down a mountainside.

goethite A black, brown or yellow mineral found in rocks.

haematite A black or grey mineral found in rocks.

harpoon A barbed, spear-like weapon, attached to a rope or wire.

Ice Age A long period of time when ice covered large parts of the Earth.

manganese A greyish-white metal found in rocks.

mine shaft A vertical tunnel leading from the surface of the ground to deep under the ground.

ochre A type of clay, ranging in colour from pale yellow to orange and red.

peat bog A wet, waterlogged area formed from mosses and other plants that have rotted down very slowly.

predator An animal that hunts and eats other animals for food.

recruit To find a suitable person for a particular job.

ritual Part of a religious ceremony.

sacred Somewhere or something that is very special and is usually connected to religion.

silicone A rubbery material.

stag A male deer.

tissues Group of cells of a similar type that come together to perform a function such as muscle tissue or bone tissue.

tomb A place where a dead body is placed.

turf A block or piece of earth with grass and plant roots, used for covering a roof.

Further Information

Websites
www.bbc.co.uk/guides/z34djxs#zgkj7ty
A BBC Bitesize guide to living, hunting and creating cave art in the Stone Age.

www.britishmuseum.org/learning/schools_and_teachers/resources/cultures/prehistoric_britain.aspx
Information and artefacts from prehistoric Britain and beyond.

www.creswell-crags.org.uk/
See if you could survive in the Stone Age by visiting the Cresswell Crags website.

www.english-heritage.org.uk/learn/story-of-england/prehistory/
Explore English Heritage's prehistory website.

www.orkneyjar.com/history/skarabrae/
Read the fascinating story of the discovery of Skara Brae on Orkney.

Books
Britain in the Past: Bronze Age by Moira Butterfield (Franklin Watts, 2015)
Found! Bronze Age by Moira Butterfield (Franklin Watts, 2017)
Explore!: Stone, Bronze and Iron Ages by Sonya Newland (Wayland, 2015)
Horrible Histories: Savage Stone Age by Terry Deary (Scholastic, 2017)

Index

Writing History

Series contents lists

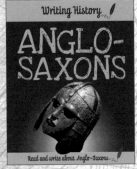

ANGLO-SAXONS
Who were the Anglo-Saxons?
Anglo-Saxon life
Kings and kingdoms
Beliefs and culture
Anglo-Saxons at war
Glossary
Further information
Index

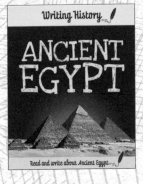

ANCIENT EGYPT
Who were the ancient Egyptians?
Ancient Egyptian life
Pharaohs and wars
Gods and beliefs
Death and the afterlife
Glossary
Further information
Index

IRON AGE
What was the Iron Age?
Iron Age life
Gods and beliefs
Telling tales
War and warriors
Glossary
Further information
Index

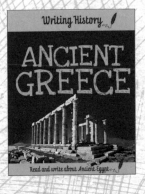

ANCIENT GREECE
Who were the ancient Greeks?
Ancient Greek life
Myths and beliefs
Learning and leisure
Greeks at war
Glossary
Further information
Index

BRONZE AGE
What was the Bronze Age?
All about bronze
Bronze Age life
Trade and transport
Burial and sacred places
Glossary
Further information
Index

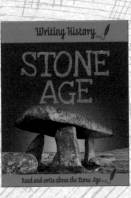

STONE AGE
What was the Stone Age?
Life in the Stone Age
Finding food
Arts and crafts
Stone Age beliefs
Glossary
Further information
Index